TESTIMONIALS

Dogs make life better. Everyone knows that. But some dogs show us how to live—with boundless curiosity, unbridled exuberance, and an irrepressible appetite for adventure. That's the story artist Dee Dee Murry tells in this charming story of a compassionate woman, a blind dachshund, and the countless empty canvases they filled with love.

~ Martin J. Smith, journalist, editor, teacher and award winning author.

I had the pleasure of meeting Hallie later in life when she needed my help as an Internal Medicine Specialist. I worked with her family to support and maintain her good quality of life. It was always a pleasure to see Hallie. She was loving and sweet, always happy to give kisses and snuggle with me and my team during her visits. One of Hallie's paintings hangs in my office. It is a testament to the soul of a truly special patient.

~ Dr. Joshua Elliott, MA, DVM, DACVIM.

The love between a human and a pet is an extraordinary experience that has the potential to change one's life in unimaginable ways. Such is the deeply enriching and touching story of Hallie, the blind dachshund who learns to paint, and her devoted human and artistic mom, Dee Dee. Their story of triumph in the face of adversity will open a tender place within your heart. Not only do they each flourish despite obstacles, but they find a way in which to give back to dogs in need, and forever and positively change the lives of countless others – both canine and human. There is nothing the human spirit can't do with a furry friend as your guide and champion!

~ Barbara Techel, award-winning author of Frankie the Walk 'N Roll Dog book series, three memoirs about the human-animal bond, and oracle card reader & intuitive guide.

In the early days of filming for The Million Dollar Duck documentary I was looking through Duck Stamp artist Rebekah Nastav's photos from previous competitions. In one group photo I noticed a woman holding a longhaired dachshund which instantly piqued my curiosity. Rebekah informed me that this was Dee Dee Murry, who never went anywhere without her beloved dog, Hallie, and to top it off Hallie could not only paint -- but was blind as well. I'd never heard of a painting dog, much less a blind one, and after seeing Dee Dee's artistic skills I knew that they would be a perfect fit for the film. Luckily Dee Dee agreed to take part, and I was excited to get the opportunity to film both her and Hallie painting in real life. It's not everyday that you get to witness a blind painting dog and master artist in action, but it was the love between them that struck me the most. The fact that Dee Dee trained Hallie to paint as a way to strengthen her mental health against blindness is truly an act of love. I'm so grateful that I got a chance to showcase this unique companionship in the documentary so that millions of people could see their story. Although I do have one regret when it comes to the Duck Stamp art competition, I still think Hallie should have entered.

~ Brian Davis, Independent Film Maker, director of the award-winning documentary, "Million Dollar Duck."

This magnificent love story is no Tall Tale, it really happened! Marvel at how author and artist Dee Dee Murry's creative dedication to her blind dachshund Hallie, provided funding for the rescue of countless other dachshunds.

~ Kizzie Jones, Author, "How Dachshunds Came to Be: A Tall Tale About a Short Long Dog."

for Hallie

my little angel in a furry
suit who blessed me with
untold wisdom, joy and
unconditional love.

HEART DOG PUBLISHING
www.heartdogpublishing.com

Puppy Picasso

The true story of a little blind dog who could paint

story and photos by Hallie's Mom
Dee Dee Murry

SHELTER

It's funny how your path in life can change in one unexpected moment. For me, it was a phone call one morning, from a friend who worked at an animal shelter.

"Guess what was dumped in the drop-off kennel last night," she said.

Oh no...don't say it.

"Three dachshunds!"

She said it!

I groaned. She knew I would be tempted. It had been 4 years since I had lost my longhaired dachshund, Jessie. She encompassed my world and the pain of losing her had been almost unbearable. I had been miserable without a dog but kept telling myself it was much preferable to giving away your heart only to have it ripped out and returned riddled with holes in the end. So, I had stood fast.

"They are surrounded by big, barking dogs!"

Oh...

"They are scared."

My...

"They need a foster home until their hold time is up and we can get them spayed and neutered."

"GEEZ! Why do you tell me these things?" I fell into my usual diatribe of why I couldn't have a dog. I'm not home enough, I have no bowls, beds, toys....

"OK fine, let them spend the next 2 weeks surrounded by barking dogs, trembling in a cold steel cage!"

By the time I came to my senses, I was already driving to the animal shelter.

Kennel #1 - Where the pups were dropped off during the night.

Inside Kennel #1

We walked down between the rows of kennels, each one held a dog with a story to tell. An elderly white dog with wire hair, cringing at the back of its cage. A shepherd mix, spittle flying from its mouth as it lunged and retreated, with tail tucked and teeth flashing.

Then there were the 3 little dachshund faces, lined up at the front of their cage, staring expectantly down the aisle. I couldn't see the back half of them, but the way their front ends were wiggling, I knew there were 3 furiously wagging tails just out of sight.

Kennel where I first saw the three pups.

The male with the smooth red coat and one blue eye sat up as we approached and perched there with a silly smile on his face. Next to him was a darling little red female with silky hair and curls down her ears. My Jessie had been a red longhair also, bigger than this tiny girl, but still so similar. My heart swelled.

Then my eyes met those of the third dachshund, a little bigger than the red girl but with a black and tan coat. Time stopped at that moment and we shared something electric. A feeling of déjà vu hit me like a yellow jacket on a mission and I knew I was in trouble.

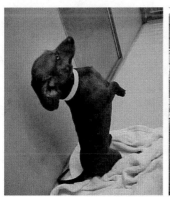

That is how I came to be driving home with a crate full of 3 wiggling pups in the back of my van and wondering what in the world just happened.

SETTLING IN

When we got home, they all tumbled pell-mell out of the crate and into the back yard, rolling the smell of the shelter off their coats in the cool grass and peeing every few feet, claiming the yard as theirs. I felt this was not right, these three in Jessie's yard. But it also healed a tiny part of my tattered soul and brought a smile to my face.

I was able to give them a closer inspection and found them to be full of fleas, dirty teeth, and nails that curled back menacingly toward their pads. Although they were not emaciated, they were too thin, and I estimated their ages at around 10 months to a year. Whatever misfortunes had befallen them in their short lives, had it been merely neglect or worse atrocities, it had not damaged their spirits.

All three were bold and playful, exploring every inch of the yard and running excitedly back to me so I could revel in their discoveries with them.

As I watched, three separate personalities emerged.

The male was the goofy big brother. His attention span didn't venture farther than what was right in front of him and he wore a perpetual smile.

The little red girl was the Event Organizer, making sure everyone was in their proper place at the proper time. And was always available to answer any questions that might arise.

Then there was the black and tan girl. She was the nurturer. A motherly presence, in charge of keeping the mood light. If things got tense, she would get silly and run zoomies in wide circles as if to tell the others to lighten up, everything would be OK. She didn't have a mean bone in her body and seemed to have a soulful wisdom lurking just behind her thoughtful brown eyes. I had fallen in love with all three dogs pretty much immediately, but when they came racing into the house from outside, I secretly hoped the black and tan girl would reach me before the others, so I could give her the first hug. I felt a connection to her that couldn't be explained and felt like it extended far back in time.

They were going to need names instead of numbers, so I temporarily dubbed them Houdini Weenie (boy), Linguini Weenie (red girl), and Zucchini Weenie (black and tan girl). Once we could get them spayed, neutered, and recovered, I wanted to get them to their new homes before I got even more attached, so I didn't waste any time starting the search. I must have made over 100 phone calls looking for the perfect homes and made lists for the best matches for each of them. I tried to disengage myself from them emotionally but only someone with a heart of stone could have resisted their charms. I finally just surrendered to the inevitable and let myself experience some of the joy I hadn't felt since losing Jessie.

Eventually, the hold time passed, and the surgeries were done. I was now faced with having to make final decisions on homes and the heartbreaking chore of letting them go. I was still adamant to not keep one and go through the eventual pain of losing them again. So I made my choices.

I found a local home for Houdini with a family of 3. He was to be an only dog but would have a stay-at-home Mom to cater to him. I knew he would love being the center of attention. His name would change to "Sam".

Little red Linguini, who was about to become "Sophie", was to go to some dear friends in Iowa. I knew she would be cherished and spoiled all her days and she had a big brother waiting for her. A black and tan longhaired Dachshund named Stormy. It was worth the long plane ride to deliver her to her new home.

Even though I knew Sophie was going to have the best family a dog could hope for, it was one of the hardest things I have ever done to leave her. I cried all the way home on the plane, knowing I was now faced with letting go of Zucchini, who had the strongest hold on my heart. There were no other homes on my list locally that even came close to my requirements for Zucchini. So I had chosen a home in Texas for her, a husband and wife who had another longhaired Dachshund that needed a friend. I had a plane ticket to fly with her to Texas 2 days later. But about three-quarters of the way through the long tearful flight home from Iowa, I had realized she would stay with me.

And I truly believe she had known that all along.

When I walked in the door from the airport, Zucchini ran over and reached her paws up to me. I scooped her up and she immediately threw her head across my shoulder and lay there, breathing softly into my neck, which was the first of what would become her famous "Hallie hugs" that she gave out freely and often, but only to me.

In the next few weeks I drove my family and friends crazy as I adjusted to the fact that I had a DOG. I wasn't going to do that ever again. Had I lost my mind? I would be lying if I said I didn't panic and pick up the phone a few times, searching again for that perfect local home to reverse what seemed like an impetuous decision to keep her. But there was no fighting the larger plan that had been set in motion that she and I were destined to belong to each other.

Sometimes during my panicked moments, Zucchini would lay her chin on my leg, roll her eyes up to me and sigh. It was as if she were telling me to hurry up and get past the stress and fear so we could get on with things. Sure enough, with each retrieve of the ball, kiss on the cheek, adoring look, and soft deep breath as she snuggled close to me at night, sharing her dreams with the twitching feet of puppy Charades, she chipped away at my carefully braced wall more and more. Until one day it crumbled, and I forgot to be afraid.

DAD

Choosing a name for your child, whether it be the two or four-legged variety, is a surprisingly daunting task. Many possibilities filled a list in my head and I tried them out periodically to no avail. So she remained Zucchini the Weenie for a time.

To give my stepmother a much-needed break, we would often go visit my Dad, my best friend, whose life was slowly being erased at the hand of Alzheimer's. Zucchini would settle into his lap with her nose to his face and a palpable peace would settle over him. Some days Dad would "be" there more than others. I treasured the days he was more present and could play our usual game of cards and tell stories yet again of the past.

Then there were the days when a lost look would cloud his eyes and he'd ask if he knew me. Zucchini comforted us both for different, but equal, reasons.

 It was one of these "lost" days when I sat with him and even though I knew it wasn't registering much, I kept up a conversation hoping to awaken something deep in his brain. But I was talking only to his presence and got no response.

I decided to run my list of puppy names past him. There had been a time he would have enjoyed helping with the decision but as I named off the contenders, he continued staring blankly ahead at nothing.

Whitney
Willow
Jasmine
Zookie
Maddie
Hallie...

The second the name was out of my mouth, Dad loudly proclaimed "HALLELUJAH!"
And thus, Hallie Hallelujah was christened.

Hallie met my onslaught of repressed motherly love with gleeful abandon. It was wonderful having a precious little being to love and spoil again and she was more than happy to reap the benefits.

She had a scar across her nose that caused the hair to come in white and I kissed it every time I asked her to "give me a Hallie Hug", wishing I could have been there to comfort her when the injury happened and hoped at least someone was.

Although she seemed happy, she spent a fair amount of time staring out the front window, ears pricking up with each car that went by, watching for someone or something familiar to her. She accepted my comforting words with appreciation and a tail wag but kept her vigil. Slowly she spent more time keeping tabs on me than what was on the other side of the glass.

Until one day, I realized she was no longer looking *for* something, but *at* something. It was then I felt she truly let go of her past.

The first order of business was to remodel the house for her. Dachshunds are notorious for the dreaded IVDD (Intervertebral Disc Disease), a premature hardening of the discs that cushion the vertebrae, making them prone to herniation and rupture. Roughly 25% of dachshunds will suffer from this painful and potentially debilitating disease, including my Jessie. I wanted to do all I could to help Hallie avoid the same fate.

The stairs to the back yard were converted into a ramp to minimize any jarring of her spine. Of course, being a wild young dog, she would sometimes come flying in from the yard, launch airborne a few feet in front of the ramp, and land halfway up before tearing into the house to complete crazy laps around the living room, smiling all the way. I developed a nervous twitch in my eye and could almost feel a few more strands of my hair turn white! Some strategically placed boxes slowed her ascent and she learned to take the ramp more slowly.

A window was installed at ground level in the living room so she could survey her reign of the neighborhood at a lower vantage point without having to risk jumping up and down off furniture. On walks, she learned that waiting for help rather than jumping off a curb was much faster and easier than enduring a hyperventilating Mother and ensuing 5 minutes of gentle reminders why we don't jump off curbs on our own. And one must never leap straight up, play tug, or make sharp turns while chasing a toy. Four on the floor is the dachshund mantra.

OBEDIENCE

Jessie and I had enjoyed competing in obedience, earning the #1 position in the Hound Group in the US with multiple all breed High in Trials. A very respectable accomplishment for a dachshund! So I decided to give it a try with Hallie also and we enrolled in classes. To my delight, she loved training and loved competing even more. At shows, she performed with precision and happy animation at every trial.

Except for one. Our very first time in the Novice ring, we were in line and ready to start, she sat in heel position at my side and stared up at me with rapt attention. When the judge said "forward!" I expected Hallie to snap into her usual prance at my side and follow my every move per the judge's commands as she always did in practice. She must have felt my tension because instead, she reverted back to her mood lifting zoomies that always worked on her two siblings, immediately bolting straight across the ring at lightning speed, cornering at the other end and turning back like a fighter jet completing its flight pattern with no intentions of landing.

I stared in shock as she made several passes at full speed, tongue lolling and short stubby feet pounding the ground. She even had the audacity to give me some low growls every time she flew by me, an invitation to join in on the game.

Visions of our careful training and daily practice over the last several months fast-forwarded through my mind in sharp contrast to the spectacle before me of my grinning puppy gone rogue. I frantically searched my mental dog training library for the best way to handle the situation with the least amount of damage to our training. But the sight of her overcome by joy with ears flapping up and down like a woman shaking out a fringed rug doubled me over in a fit of laughter. We may have failed the trial but what we took home that day was worth much more than any ribbon.

FASHION MODEL

I first entered the world of photography when Hallie was a young dog and she became a willing test subject while I learned the ropes. She was rewarded with lots of treats and praise during her photo sessions, which were kept short and fun, and relished her time in front of the camera. She would come strutting out to the middle of the set like a Vegas showgirl and start striking poses.

Her wardrobe took up more drawers in the dresser than mine did. If she had been my human daughter instead of my four-legged hairy one, I am sure her spending habits at the malls would have forced me into bankruptcy. She loved being dressed up, no matter how intricate the outfit, and would spin circles when I started to bring out her clothes. She had the patience of a saint and would hold a pose for as long as I needed, even leaning slightly to balance a hat or pair of sunglasses on her head.

She made me laugh so much in her various adornments, I began creating scenes of her in Photoshop and putting them on calendars and cards. Each year the design of our Christmas card got more and more elaborate, and as the years went by, harder to come up with new ideas.

Which is how she eventually became a Christmas peacock and an entire dysfunctional family of anthropomorphic wiener dogs.

HALLIEday Greetings!

Merry Christmas!

Grandpa Dad Mom Zucchini Linguini

Hope your Christmas is Picture Perfect!

Dee Dee and Hallie

a healthy and happy New Year

Dee Dee and Hallie

Hallie-lujah!

CRITTERS

Hallie was the sweetest soul I've ever met. She did not display any of her Dachshund heritage as a badger hunter. If thrown into a den of them, she would have walked around handing out cold beverages and making sure everyone was comfortable. Baby chicks burrowed underneath her soft black coat. Rabbits, squirrels, kittens.... everything was to be mothered and nurtured.

Horses, on the other hand, had a very impolite way of blowing hot air into her face, making her backpedal in my arms with wide indignant eyes. Then look at me as if she expected me to teach them some horse/dog etiquette. We learned to respect her personal bubble when meeting horses. Just out of horse breath reach.

photo by Gwyn Servey

FEDERAL DUCK STAMP

Everywhere I went, Hallie was always by my side. If she couldn't go, I didn't go. Being a pet and wildlife artist, we often went to farms to photograph horses or traipsing into the woods with my camera to capture images of animals to paint.

Many of these excursions involved finding and photographing waterfowl. I enter the Federal Duck Stamp competition every year. As the only juried art competition run by the U.S. government, the winning duck stamp helps raise millions of dollars to conserve wetland habitat for waterfowl, fish, and other wildlife. In the art world, winning the contest is comparable to winning an Academy Award. So I needed good photos to use as reference for my painting.

Hallie's first time in the field with me was to a hidden pond where waterfowl often flock in large numbers. We hiked the mile in, struggling through wet brush and slippery rocks, often with Hallie in one arm and my camera in the other while trying to remain upright.

Ducks tend to be skittish so need to be approached as inconspicuously as possible. I was impressed that Hallie seemed to sense our need for stealth as she calmly followed close in my footsteps and paused when I did. Finally, we settled ourselves into some bushes on the bank of the pond, and I tied her leash to my ankle. We sat looking out onto water, rich with several species of ducks that I needed to photograph. Slowly, I raised my camera to my eye and focused on a beautiful Mallard drake floating languidly on the surface.

Before I could click the shutter, there was an explosion of wings, water, and quacking ducks! My first thought was there must be a hunter out there with us, when suddenly my foot was jerked forward and I about dropped my lens. Hallie had run the length of the 10-foot leash and splashed into the water, sending the ducks flurrying skyward.

We now sat in front of an empty pond, my jaw hanging open and Hallie staring up at the sky in full point. She turned and met my gaze with questioning eyes as if the sudden departure of the ducks was somehow my fault and could I please get them back for her. The sight of her innocent look and dripping coat made me burst out laughing and we started the long hike back down the hill. The ducks would not be back that day.

THE BEACH

One of the many gifts Hallie brought me was rekindling my interest in exploring. We made time for trips to the mountains, rain forest, ballet, Monastery, flower gardens, antique shopping, horse shows, movies, concerts, art galleries.... all things I would have not taken the time to do by myself.

But our favorite place on earth was the beach!

When I set her down on the soft sand for the very first time, I had no idea what her reaction would be and watched expectantly. At first, she stood stock still, staring toward the crashing waves. Then with no warning, lunged forward at full tilt, sending sand flying in her wake. I did my best to keep up at leash length, wanting her to fully enjoy her first experience at the beach as unhampered by the leash and my slow human legs as possible. She steered me at high speed through 3 children building a sandcastle, over driftwood, and into a flock of seagulls who rose to the air screaming indecencies down at us.

Finally, she noticed a guided group of tourists on horses going by and stopped to evaluate the situation while I bent to catch my breath. As they moved down the beach she made her way over to their tracks without taking her eyes off them, still not knowing what to make of these odd horse-humans.

Until she realized what she was standing on.

Fresh horse droppings littered the ground in front of her, something she had never encountered. Before I could pull her away she grabbed one, immediately made a face, shook her head, and let go, sending it flying across the sand and hitting an innocent bystander in the bare calf. The man looked around with a frown, and not noticing the offending object, turned back to his family.

An inner battle of emotions fought in Hallie's head, alternating between the urge to pick one up and then, overwhelmed by disgust, would shake her head and let it fly. Some of the pieces fell harmlessly to the sand but others found their mark on the unsuspecting family members.

Unfortunately, the first one to realize what was happening was a little girl. And as little girls do, let out an ear-piercing shriek.

"POO POO!!!" she began to wail, frantically shaking her hands in a "get it off me" motion.

While the parents were trying to figure out what had upset the little girl, I pulled Hallie to a small group of seniors sitting together in their beach chairs and braided sun hats and joined them in staring at the family, appearing to be as dumbfounded as they were.

"Seagull must have pooped on her head," we heard an older gentleman say gruffly as we walked away.

PRESENTS and HOLIDAYS

Thankfully I'm blessed with family and friends, who either shared, or if not, at least tolerated my devotion to a four-legged family member and treated Hallie as such. To me, she was as much my child as if she had been human. I am glad to see the world slowly (albeit a little too slowly in some areas) beginning to accept the importance of pets as family. I know there are a lot of people out there who feel the same way.

On holidays, Hallie would receive many gifts which she quickly learned to open on her own, preferring to savor tearing each piece of paper off the box until she finally got to the real treasure. She would give each gift its fair due before moving on to the next and wait until the end to choose her favorites.

At 12 lbs she was a small dog but most people who didn't live near us and hadn't seen her in person, typically underestimated her size, sending her jackets that fit more like hats and collars that fit my wrist better than her neck. We just got creative and repurposed each gift.

One Christmas we were at a pet store and I told her she could pick out anything she wanted. Of course, she didn't understand, but ran wagging through the store at the end of her leash nosing everything at dachshund nose level. Finally, she spotted a big gray donut bed sized for a Great Dane and hopped in. When I tried to call her out, she planted herself and wouldn't budge. The store clerk laughed and came over with treats to lure her out. But the more we cajoled, the cuter she got, finally sitting up in the air and waving her front paws at us.

After the clerk took a photo to post on the store bulletin board, I sighed and said I guess we'll take it.

$80 and many years later she never set foot in that bed again.

SCHUTZHUND

The sport of Schutzhund was originally developed in Germany to test the skill and working aptitude of the German Shepherd dog. Today the competition is open to any breed, but working breeds are most commonly seen in trials, such as Belgian Malinois, Rottweilers, Dobermans, Pit Bulls, German Shepherds and the like. In other words, the "bodybuilders" of the dog world.

Schutzhund incorporates exercises similar to what Police Dogs are trained to do. Apprehending a criminal (referred to as a "decoy" in a Schutzhund trial) by chasing the subject, flying through the air, and latching onto their arm which is covered in a heavy burlap sleeve. Scaling a tall wall to retrieve a dumbbell. And being asked to execute a series of vigorous obedience exercises to test the temperament and stability of the dog.

A friend of ours was very active and successful in the sport of Schutzhund with her Pit Bulls. We often went to watch and photograph the dogs in action. The first level of competition is the BH. Although it was more rigorous than the AKC obedience trials we were used to, I wondered if Hallie and I might be able to earn this basic Schutzhund title. There would be no jumping or bite work at this level, so no jarring to her delicate dachshund back but the heeling exercises were significantly longer and covered a lot more ground than AKC, especially when your legs were just a fraction of the height of the other dogs entered.

So with the help of our friend and the local Schutzhund club, we set to work.

After weeks of training, we arrived at the event grounds to dark skies and pouring rain. This was not a good sign as, although Hallie was quite tolerant of just about anything, she was pretty sure she could melt in the rain. And this was supposed to be fun, not a chore. I would be watching her for signs of quitting and not push her too far.

I put on her fleece jacket and we went over to check-in, huddling next to the propane heater while waiting our turn. We were finally called and walked out onto the field, looking like a mismatched circus act. She in her red plaid jacket and me in my purple coat. I could almost hear the big dogs snickering from the sidelines.

The judge was flown in from Germany and had a very thick accent. He couldn't pronounce her name well, so he just called her "Low Dog." We followed his direction and approached the group of people that we were to heel around. The rain had shown us no mercy and soaked us through, removing any bit of dignity we had left. But we made a good start, Hallie prancing by my side in perfect position, giving me her rapt attention with her eyes focused on mine.

But everyone has their limit. Hallie decided she would play along and give her all for a precise amount of time. Which happened to be maybe 3.5 minutes.

Then I saw a familiar look cross her face and in retrospect, should have just headed back to our van right then.

Sure enough, she lost all abandon, donned a goofy grin, and cavorted on ahead, leaving me alone in the rain. She did a half zoomie and circled back behind me while I kept moving forward on the pattern as if we were both still heeling. I called her and pointed to heel position by my side as a reminder to where she was supposed to be. When that didn't work, I pointed with two fingers. Then three. Then five. I turned to see how far behind me she was and found her a few yards back, peeing in a squatting position.

The rain was coming down harder and I hoped maybe the judge couldn't see clearly from the distance. I was starting to giggle and about ready to pull out the white flag and take her out for ice cream when something shifted in her and she ran over to finish the pattern in perfect position.

When it was all over, we joined the others for award presentation just to thank the judge and to congratulate the ones that passed.

Imagine my surprise to learn that "Low Dog" had passed by a hair and was the proud new owner of a Schutzhund title!

GOING BLIND

With each year that passed, time gathered the new memories we made and wove them tightly into the ever-deepening bond between us. Hallie was now 10 years old and although starting to show a little frost on the pumpkin, was as spry and active as she'd always been. It was the end of March and we had just spent a wonderful weekend at the beach, walking the boardwalk, running in the sand and nestling up against a large piece of driftwood to watch the sun sink into the low laying clouds and then out of sight.

We started the 2 1/2 hour drive home and fell into bed exhausted, sleeping in longer than usual the next morning which was, ironically, April Fool's Day. When we got up, I noticed Hallie did not seem as animated to get her breakfast as she usually was. Concern washed over me.

Did she eat something at the beach? Is her back going out?

I deflected the possibilities my brain was throwing at me and watched her. Hopefully it was just another case of overactive worried mother syndrome. After all, I wasn't even sure it was that unusual, given the long trip she could just be a bit tired yet. But when I put her food bowl down and my normally voracious girl just stood there not moving, all bells and sirens went off and I was immediately in full panic.

I picked up a piece of her food and tossed it onto the floor in front of her to see if she would eat but she still didn't move or acknowledge the morsel. I carried her to her bowl and, nose twitching, she dove right in.

That was very odd. I watched her clean up the bowl, and as she started to walk away, bump into the edge of the fridge.

Thank goodness I was already dressed, or I would have shown up at the Veterinary Clinic with my pajamas on. We saw our longtime Vet, Dr. Sparling, who confirmed what was obvious. Hallie could not see! But we didn't know the cause. I prayed it was cataracts, something we could fix. But Hallie would need further testing to get a diagnosis. Dr. Sparling referred us to a board-certified veterinary ophthalmologist who got us in the next day.

Running on little sleep and an energy drink, we drove the 2 hours to the clinic. All the way there, I visualized the Ophthalmologist telling us it was just cataracts and pictured myself driving home with a smile born of relief, knowing we could do surgery and she would be able to see again. But once the Vet completed his exam, he gave me the news. SARDS. Sudden Acquired Retinal Degeneration Syndrome. He told me SARDS had minimal treatment options and no cure.

I had never heard of this disease. But I later learned that of the dogs that get this, among the most common are spayed female Dachshunds with allergies...all of which Hallie was. It is an autoimmune disease where the body attacks its own retinas, causing complete blindness very quickly. Often SARDS dogs have increased hunger and thirst in the weeks before the blindness hits, but Hallie did not. Looking back, the only signs I saw were tearing of one eye, unequal pupil size due to unrelated iris atrophy, and not reacting to a white cat that had run through our yard after dark one night. None of which seemed terribly concerning at the time.

Even though I knew searching the internet for SARDS would push me right over the thin edge of composure I was standing on, I booted up the computer as soon as we got home. Most of the information was dour. But then I came across an article about a SARDS researcher at Iowa State University who was having some success at restoring SARDS dogs' vision. It sounded very controversial and the procedure was risky. But reading things like "Blind Dogs Now Cured with SARDS!" and "Researchers Find Cure for Dogs with SARDS" it was impossible to not try.

There is just a small window of time for treatment to be successful. Once the retinas are too damaged, which can happen quite quickly, the procedure would not work. The ophthalmologist had said Hallie's retinas still looked normal. I immediately called the researcher at Iowa State. Although we were able to make an appointment, he was out of the office for 3 weeks. I white knuckled my way through the interim, praying her retinas would still be viable by the time he could see her.

Finally the 3 weeks were up. Hallie weathered the long plane ride to Iowa like a trooper, snuggling into my lap for a snooze even with the loud noises and rumbling beneath us. I was so thankful for my stepmother to be taking the trip with us. She was much needed support.

The only bright side of this trip was the University was very near to our friends home where I had delivered her sister almost a decade earlier! So while we waited for our appointment at the University, we went to our friends to reunite the sisters. Tears filled my eyes when I saw Sophie, (FKA Linguini). She had matured into a beautiful little lady with a now frosted face. She too was having sight issues with cataracts. But it was wonderful to see in person how obviously spoiled, loved and treasured she had been all these years as I knew she would be! I had always said the only way I would fly anywhere with Hallie would be if she were ill and there was only one Vet in the world that could help her. I never dreamed that day would actually come true. So it never crossed my mind that Hallie and her sister Sophie would ever meet again. What a wonderful visit we had with our friends and watching the girls together again!

We left early the next morning for Hallie's appointment at the University. But her exam showed her retinas were far too damaged for his procedure to work so there was nothing the researcher could do. I went through an entire box of kleenex as he delivered the news. I honestly thought our world had ended.

We returned home crushed. I was sure life would never be happy for us again. Her sudden loss of vision made for a more jarring adjustment than if it had been gradual and I was determined to protect her from the things I still could at all costs.

I padded the house inside and out with pillows and pool noodles, strung caution tape along pathways to help guide her, and removed chairs and tables from the house so she wouldn't hit her head on the legs.

I was obsessed with creating the perfect bumper hat to protect her head if she were to run into things. I am not sure how much they helped really, and we abandoned the idea in the end, but she wore them stoically.

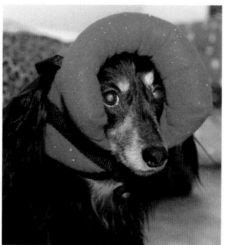

Then we hunkered down, swaddled in our inner sanctum of "safety" so as not to let any more demons in, and didn't leave the house for weeks. I failed miserably at keeping a "happy attitude."

As it turned out, isolating her at home was the worst thing I could have done. And after a while, Hallie let me know that she was not about to give up living just because of this little bump in the road.

Together we ventured out to our old stomping grounds. Every day I would set her down and if there were sounds like wind, traffic, or a flapping flag, she would freeze in place and shake. She could hear the movement but didn't know where it was coming from. She refused to walk but that was OK. I was letting her set the pace for everything and would just sit with her until she relaxed. It was several days before she took that first step on her own.

Then came the day when she suddenly broke into a RUN. I would have done a cartwheel if I had not been approaching the age I could easily break a hip, so I ran along with her, holding the leash taut as straight up as I could so if she did stumble, she wouldn't hit her nose on the ground. Trust was everything in gaining her confidence and I wasn't about to shake that by letting her get hurt.

Before long she often made me forget she was blind. Every time we got out of the car and I set her down, she would stand very still for 1 or 2 minutes, taking it all in. Then she would take off at a run and I'd pinwheel along with her, steering her around drain grates and bumps, until she suddenly screeched to a halt. She would wait again then take off without warning and so would go our walks. Always with a big smile on both of our faces.

I wasn't sure if it was the best idea, but finally, we returned to the ocean. I was afraid the elements that made her love the beach so much before, may now be a harsh bombardment on the senses she still had. But the minute she felt the sand sifting through her toes, she was off like the puppy who used to sling poop balls at people, wearing that endearing grin she always got doing what she loved best.

I knew this would be the first of many more wonderful trips to the beach!

NOSEWORK

I heard about a new dog sport called K9 Nosework and a friend suggested I try it with Hallie. I had not yet learned Hallie's lesson that she could do pretty much anything she set her mind to, so I didn't give it a second thought. But I discovered a class with great instructors and supportive classmates, who were wonderful about letting Hallie do what she could at her own pace.

It was life-changing for us. It is all about the dogs using their noses, which Hallie was an expert at by then, having to rely on her sense of smell to navigate her world. A scented Q Tip is hidden in different scenarios such as a room, on a vehicle, in boxes, and outdoors. The dog must find the "hide" in each of these locations and indicate to its handler where it is. It is great fun for both the handler and the dog, and for Hallie, it was something for the first time since going blind that she was in control of.

She didn't need any help to find the hide and in fact, got a little put off if I did try to help. This was her game and she did it very well.

Once the hide was placed, I would set Hallie on the ground and let her take stock of her surroundings with her nose for several seconds. You could see it twitching and bending to the left and the right as she pulled in the smells from the search area while her brain processed and separated each odor in her mind. Then I would say "Find it!" and she would bound forward, all business with tail wagging in anticipation and follow wherever her nose took her. It was fascinating to watch her work an area, being led by odor we couldn't begin to detect, her head going up and down, then checking herself as she caught the scent and doubling back to hone in on it.

Nothing stopped her even when she would bump into a box or wall, she would just change direction and keep following her nose. We called her the Hallie Roomba.

I remember early in her training, she located a hide in a box and when we all cheered and clapped for her, she did a happy little spin. I had not seen that spin since before she went blind. It was the best feeling ever.

We eventually started to go to Nosework trials where the dogs are timed and required to find the hide in all four areas (or "elements") in the same day. Hallie earned her NW1 title coming in 8th out of 33 sighted dogs and won the coveted Harry Award, which is given to the most outstanding rescue dog that demonstrates extraordinary ability and spirit in nose work at the NW1 level. I couldn't have been more proud!

With Dorothy Turley, one of our amazing Nosework instructors who, along with Rachelle Bailey-Austin, so kindly guided Hallie and I through our classes and made this possible for us.

PAINTING

I kept Hallie's mind and body busy so she would be happy to rest at home. I didn't want her to lay there bored in her darkness with nothing to do. So on a snowy day in January, when it was too cold to venture out even for a walk, I began to dream up some new tricks to teach her. Since I make my living as an artist, I thought maybe I could teach her to paint. If it didn't go anywhere that was OK. The point was for her to have fun learning something new.

As with all her training, she was never scolded or forced to do anything she didn't want to. We always kept everything fun with a lot of treats and praise. At first, it was just touching the brush handle to her lips. Then slowly asking more and more until she was holding it in her mouth. She already knew how to "target" from earlier training, where she would touch her nose to whatever object I held in front of her, so when I said "touch" she poked her head forward with the brush. I put a pen protector on the brush to help her keep a solid grasp on the handle and would set up a pad of art paper in front of her that had a lot of give to it so when she touched it with the brush, the pressure wouldn't force the brush back into her mouth.

In the beginning, we had some very entertaining blunders as she learned to pick up and hold the brush properly, and exactly what I wanted her to do with it, including some loaded brushes being launched across the room with me diving to intercept before paint hit the carpet. She also had a knack of missing the paper and painting my jeans as I sat in front of her. If I didn't know better, I would have thought she was doing it intentionally! Since all blunders were reacted to with laughter and kisses on top of her head, telling her what a silly girl she was, she never was upset when she made a "mistake" but kept happily trying until she got it right.

Eventually, I added paint to the empty jars and an artist was born! We used non-toxic children's paint, and I mixed up several jars of it in different colors, each with its own brush. I placed the jar just to her right with the brush angled toward her and she would reach down and pick it up without fail every time.

Once done with a color, I swapped the jars to another, and off she would go again. In her almost 4 years of painting, she never once decided to end a session on her own. I would always have to take the brush from her, and she'd search for it, still wanting to paint. I never wanted to push her to the point of wanting to stop. Giving her something fun to do was the main goal.

As she painted, she would get excited and wiggle around a little, inching herself away from the painting pad that she no longer could reach with the brush. So I rolled up a blanket for her to sit on to keep her in position near the pad. And of course, she needed her own artist's beret. We found a jaunty red one that she loved to wear as that was her cue we were going to get to paint!

When everything was set in place, I would sit on the floor behind the painting pad with Hallie in front of me, looking adorable in her little beret and sitting on her rolled-up blanket, waiting until I asked her to "paint!" She would reach over, pick up the brush as if she had perfect vision, and start a dabbing motion with it, often raising a front paw to feel for the paper, but with her leg being shorter than her nose and the brush, she could never reach it.

I would bend forward, encouraging and praising her while she worked and take the brush from her after every few brush strokes. Followed immediately by a treat while I told her how beautiful her painting was coming along. I discovered the better the treat, the faster she painted!

Her first painting will always occupy a treasured spot on my wall. It is called "Confetti" and looks like me with a red body and blue legs, wearing a yellow hat and holding a yellow bone. Hallie is jumping up on my leg for the bone and has a blue body with her yellow head turned to look at her red beret that has just fallen off.

It is very clear.

If you squint.

And turn your head sideways.

And maybe have a little wine first.

And it's a little unsettling that it appears she painted my intestines on the outside, but you never question an artist's vision.

GETTING FAMOUS

We started to acquire quite a stack of paintings and I wondered if there might be a way to sell them to support dog rescue. I searched for just the right rescue. I wanted one that did great work and would use every penny for the dogs. I also wanted a smaller rescue so whatever bit we donated would make a bigger difference. When I learned about Purple Heart Rescue in Chehalis, WA, I knew my search was over. They are a wonderful rescue and take in the hard-core cases, healing their often battered bodies and minds so they can be successfully integrated into wonderful forever homes. I could see their dedication and compassion to every animal that came through their doors. So, I created a web site at www.hallieart.com and put Hallie's art up for sale.

Debbie Harp and Sandy Winberry with Hallie. If you would like to donate to Purple Heart Rescue, please go to:

www.purpleheartrescue.com

Our local paper heard about the little blind dachshund who paints and came over for an interview, dubbing her "Puppy Picasso."

Which started the whole thing.

Her story circulated, and I talked with Kim Holcomb, an award-winning reporter and host who was interested in covering Hallie's story for Seattle's KING 5 TV's 'Evening Magazine'.

I was thrilled!

Then I was terrified. Especially when it hit me that I would be filmed along with Hallie! Guessing a paper bag over my head would be frowned upon, I scrambled to update my hair and clothes to the 21st century.

Hallie, a blind eleven-year-old dachshund, paints using a brush clamped between its jaws.

Chris Gaines | tgaines@chronline.com

Puppy Picasso
Paints Pictures

By Bianca Fortis
bfortis@chronline.com

The next Vincent van Gogh is living right here in Lewis County — except she is four-legged, furry and blind.

Hallie, an 11-year-old brown and black dachshund, has been painting for about a year.

Her owner, Dee Dee Murry, 51, also an artist, said Hallie would often sit on her shoulder or lay across her lap while she was painting in her studio.

One day she decided to let Hallie try. It took about two weeks to train her, Murry said.

Murry lays towels on her kitchen floor and sets up a 6-by-9 inch "easel," with a cup of children's non-toxic paint and a brush next to it.

When Murry says the word "paint," Hallie — with a little red beret perched on top of her

We went to stores, near schools, any new and busy places with unusual sounds I could find to get her used to painting in different situations. When they heard the story, some businesses even had people crowd around us to applaud and cheer for her as she painted to acclimate her to the noise. She didn't miss a beat!

I went on a search for new paint jars as the ones she had were just plastic cups and looking well worn. I wanted something the right height, that wouldn't tip over easily, with lids that would screw on tight to avoid paint spills in the car.

When we went into a store, we would fill our cart with as many jar prospects as we could find. Then we would retreat to a quiet corner, where I would lay out Hallie's painting towel, settle her on top of it, kneel to the floor in front of her and start testing the different jar heights against her.

Once I found one that seemed just right, I checked it for tipping ease by setting it on the towel next to her and asking her to "paint". She would reach down and pick up the brush, then happily start painting the air.

At one point I looked up to see a young couple staring at us with their mouths open. The woman said "We are trying to figure out what you are doing!" to which I replied, "You wouldn't believe me if I told you."

Hallie painting with her friend Sammie.

When Kim Holcomb and her cameraman, Tom Bishop, pulled up in front of our house I was still a little worried, not fully knowing if having new people and different sounds of the camera would distract her while she worked.

But once I put the beret on her head she knew exactly what to do and eagerly painted for them until they got all the footage they needed. Surprisingly, I was not nervous at all. Hallie carried my courage and to have my precious girl being filmed for TV after all she had endured and overcome, overrode any fear or awkwardness. It was just her and I in our own little bubble as I sat on the other side of her painting pad, encouraging and praising her and slipping her treats after each set of strokes.

When the show aired, family and friends gathered so we could watch it together. The first sight of seeing my girl on TV seemed surreal. What an amazing little soul.

Within an hour after the show was over, sales started to come in for Hallie's art. She only had around 30 paintings up for sale at that point which I thought was a lot. But they sold out in a couple of days. Every time I put up a set of new ones, they would sell in a few hours. I was excited to have a nice check to give to the rescue!

Then one day, a friend told me they saw a clip of Hallie painting on Good Morning America. Her story had gone viral! I couldn't believe I was seeing MY Hallie featured on major web portals, television networks and dozens of celebrity and store sites.

Yahoo

ABC

Xfinity

Orvis

I checked my email later that morning to find the remaining art on her site had sold. I would upload a batch of 10 - 20 new paintings every day or so and literally within seconds, they would be gone, followed by a barrage of emails saying they missed this bunch, when would there be more? Even if it were the wee hours of the morning.

One poor woman had been sitting up at night for weeks, hitting refresh on her keyboard in the hopes of getting one but kept missing it by seconds. She finally emailed me and I told her I'd let her know when the next batch was going up so she could be ready. But even then she was never fast enough to succeed. Finally I took pity on her and held one out for her.

Hallie could knock them out pretty fast, but I never let her paint more than 10-15 minutes at a time. It was an important part of her life and I didn't want it to stop being fun for her. But that meant there was a very long wait list.

It was almost a full-time job packaging the paintings, keeping records, and shipping them out. Bless the kind people at our post office who were very patient to scan through huge stacks of paintings several times a week, taking up to 45 minutes at a time. I am sure they each hoped I wouldn't get their window when we walked in! But they never complained.

Diane and Jerry, Post Office heroes!

People started asking for Hallie to sign her paintings. I tried dipping her paw in paint and gently pressing it on the paper, but with her fuzzy paws, it would just look like a big blob. So I took a photo of her nose and had it made into a rubber stamp that I pressed into a corner of each painting with red ink to give it that final touch!

Meanwhile, the phone was ringing off the hook, and we were being asked to be on TV and Radio shows, paint at public events, her art to be on book covers, or to hang in high end restaurants, businesses and art galleries. I didn't know whose world I had just stepped into, but it was nothing like mine!

"Flame Thrower"

"Edame"

"Dragon's Lair"

"Green Bird on a Branch"

Our first time being filmed on an actual set was on New Day Northwest at KING 5 TV in Seattle. As always, Hallie acted like this was something she did every day and I was just along for the ride. Which was a good thing, because if I were doing something like that alone, I would have bolted before I got past the Green Room.

The Green Room is a quiet place where you sit and reflect on all of the stupid things you might do or say, very shortly, in front of thousands of viewers. I visualized about 10 ways I could escape the building without being seen. I wondered if I would be their first "runner." But this was Hallie's moment so I persevered!

By the time we were actually setting up and being briefed, I took a deep breath, looked into Hallie's soulful eyes and relaxed, feeling I might just get through this without embarrassing Hallie too much after all. As luck would have it, the host of the show wasn't there that day so we got Kim Holcomb who was standing in for her. It was nice to see a familiar face! She led us through the interview and deflected a few of my bloopers! But Hallie, always the consummate professional, did a great job and a successful first experience on set in front of cameras and sounds of a studio.

And a star was born!

BOB RIVERS RADIO SHOW

Bob Rivers was a great personality and a good sport! On his radio show, the staff blindfolded Bob, put a paint brush in his mouth, and had him and Hallie both paint at the same time. Then they posted the two paintings on their web site and had the public guess which was done by Bob and which was done by Hallie. The almost unanimous vote went to one of the paintings, which the public thought was Bob's as it was the better painting. When in fact, it was Hallies!

JOHN SHARIFY - KING 5 NEWS

John and his cameraman, Douglas Burgess, did a wonderful job filming Hallie, and included footage of Purple Heart Rescue. The cameraman even took a tennis ball to the face while filming. And yet kept his great attitude. This film was nominated for a local Emmy Award!

BEN BARNETT - KOMO 4 NEWS

Ben Barnett did a great job filming Hallie for KOMO 4 News in Seattle. By then, Hallie was a seasoned "performer" and most of my pre-filming jitters were gone. But I never lost my tendancy to cringe when I saw myself on TV. Thank goodness eyes were mainly on Hallie!

I was often asked if I felt Hallie was painting to express some kind of creative urge from deep within. My answer was always the same. No. She's a dog. To her it was a fun trick she had learned that got her praise, attention and most importantly, treats. It gave her life a new meaning and made her happy. And that was all that mattered.

Hallie and I were asked to be feature co-artists at art shows. But of course, everyone really came to see HER art. And I wouldn't have had it any other way. Often children would kneel in a row next to her and call out which color I should set down next for her while she was painting, some of them petting her as she did. She never wavered from her task, even with the noise and confusion. In fact, the noisier the room was, the more intently she painted. It filled my heart to think of her first few weeks being blind and too afraid to even take a step, and then to see all she did now without blinking an eye.

One exceptionally proud moment was when we found out that Hallie had won a Humanitarian Award at the PAWS Community Hero Pets Awards on Bainbridge Island, for her donations to animal rescue from the sales of her art work, and were honored to attend a banquet for the awards ceremony. Although the majority of her donations went to Purple Heart Rescue, we did donate to various other rescues and individuals that needed help. In the end, she donated over $35,000.00 to animals in need.

I had a pretty good year selling my art that year, but my blind dog sold more art than I did. I am fairly sure no one in the world has ever been able to claim that.

Centralia's Painting Dog Receives Humanitarian Award

Hallie, a blind 11-year-old dachshund, paints using a brush clamped between its jaws. The paintings are sold to raise money for charity.

DONATION: *Owner of Blind, Deaf Dachshund Gives Funds From Paintings to Purple Heart Rescue*

By Kyle Spurr
kspurr@chronline.com

Since Centralia artist Dee Dee Murry trained her blind 12-year-old Dachshund Hallie how to paint more than a year ago, the two have received national attention and recently won a Humanitarian award at the PAWS Community Hero Pets Awards on Bainbridge Island.

Hallie won the Humanitarian award for Murry's donation of all proceeds she raised from Hallie's paintings to Purple Heart Rescue, a nonprofit dog foster care program based in Chehalis.

To date, Hallie has raised more than $15,000 for the local foster care program.

Murry said Hallie, who paints about five to 10 pieces a week, has become a motivation for her to keep pursuing her own artistic career.

"I could have stayed home and been depressed with her when she went blind," Murry said. "She is inspiring to me."

Hallie suffered a sudden acquired retinal degeneration, or SARDS, which left her blind al-

most overnight last April. Murry had to retrain Hallie to paint, which consists of the dog biting down on a brush and dragging it across a canvas.

About three months ago, Murry said, Hallie also went deaf, yet has not stopped painting.

"She hasn't changed a lot and maybe she works more on her own then I realized," Murry said.

Hallie's ability to pick up a paintbrush with her mouth and dab at a blank canvas has also become an inspiration to others.

In the past year, Murry said, Hallie has been featured on King 5's Evening Magazine and New Day Northwest, KOMO News, and various radio shows. A clip of Hallie painting also made it on "Good Morning America."

Murry said she was contacted by representatives for Anderson Cooper of CNN, who asked if she could fly to New York to appear on his show, "Anderson Live."

"They said he really likes art and animals," Murry said. "We really tried to work it out, but I didn't feel comfortable flying her out there."

With all the attention and sold paintings, Murry said she doesn't use any of the money for her income. All of it goes to the Purple Heart Rescue. Murry supports herself with her own artwork and web development

skills.

"I joke that my blind dog sold more art than I did," Murry said.

Murry and Hallie are often recognized when they are out in public. Murry said she welcomes the fame but she is most satisfied with giving her dog, who was rescued, a good life.

When Hallie isn't painting, she participates in K9 Nose Work, canine classes that helps develop a dog's sense of smell.

"When she went blind I figured the rest of her life we would

just have to sit at home," Murry said. "The opposite has been true. The most important thing out of all the things she's done is not that she is more famous, but it's what she has overcome."

[Plaque text:]

PAWS
of Bainbridge Island and North Kitsap

PAWS Spotlight on Community Hero Pets

Presented for heroic service to:

Hallie

PAWS Humanitarian Award

2013

I answered a call out of a deep sleep early one morning, to find myself talking to Anderson Cooper's assistant. I am pretty sure she thought she had misdialed and reached someone at a bar as I mumbled and stumbled my way through the conversation. They wanted to fly us out to New York to be on his show! Which I would have loved to do. But at Hallie's age and health issues, I felt the trip would be more for my sake than hers and I didn't want to put her at any risk. I hated to turn down such a great opportunity. But we kept our "appearances" close to home.

Often, as I was preparing her paints on a set, she would wander about, following the footsteps of the crew and sniffing her way to the food table. More than once she would find one of her brushes on her own and I'd turn to see her sitting off by herself, painting the air.

During one interview, a cameraman got down on her level and was filming her about 10 inches away as she painted. He made a noise, so she turned her head his direction with a brush in her mouth loaded with red
paint, leaving a bright red swath across his huge, and no doubt, very expensive lens. He donned a stricken look and disappeared at a good clip to a back room.

Well...I thought it was funny.

In between being filmed and public demo's, we kept busy trying to keep up with orders. At first, I titled her paintings by what they looked like. She tended to paint a lot of hummingbirds and tulips.

But there are only so many ways to name something after a hummingbird or a tulip. So, after a few hundred paintings, I started to just make things up. And very much enjoyed watching people at her showings read the title and exclaim "Oh yes! I see it!" As they tilted their heads and pointed.

'The Running Biscuit' was one of my favorites, although nothing in the painting looked like it.

Or did it?

Her painting style changed over time, but that was due more to changing brushes and the viscosity of the paint than her changing her technique.

We got requests for interviews from several national and international magazines and publications, including National Geographic Kids magazine, and Coastal Dog. Hallie began getting gifts in the mail from school children and dog lovers from all over the world. One teacher had her entire class paint pictures with the brush in their mouths, and sent all of the paintings to us along with other wonderful treasures from the kids. I will always treasure each one. I tried to answer every email and loved getting photos and hearing about other people's dogs.

One of Hallie's paintings graces the cover of Barbara Novero Levy's wonderful book, "Be Your Pet's Best Friend."

Hallie art hanging on the wall of Momofuku Milk Bar in NYC.

So this happened one day! I don't really know how it happened. I think it started with an innocent question to my cousin who worked at a sign shop. "How much would it cost to plaster bigger than lifesized Hallie images on our van?" It was largely said in jest. But when I found out what a good deal I could get on it, how could I refuse? I figured if nothing else, it wouldn't get stolen. I could imagine the APB announcement.

"Be on the look out for a 1992 maroon Mercury Villager with very large weiner dogs on either side, wearing hats and holding a rose."

Guessing they wouldn't get very far.

One day I got an email from an independent filmmaker, Brian Davis, asking if I would like to be part of a documentary he would be filming on the Federal Duck Stamp competition. The film was to follow the journey of 6 artists as they prepared, painted, and sent off their duck stamp entries to the competition. I was asked partly because of Hallie, partly because of my Federal Duck Stamp entries over the years and partly because I would be the only one in the group who did not and never would hunt a duck. I felt very honored to be asked and of course, said yes! Although it seemed a little strange to be part of a show for the first time that wasn't focused solely on Hallie.

It was great fun being filmed that summer and seeing how something like this was put together.

Hallie and I, with Brian Davis (director) and Christian Bruno (cinematographer).

Being an independent film, there was no guarantee it would be picked up and aired anywhere. But at the world premiere at Slam Dance Film Festival in Park City, Utah, it was a big hit, receiving the coveted Audience Award for Best Documentary Feature as well as the Jury Award for Documentary Feature.

It was immediately picked up by both Animal Planet and Lion's Gate Entertainment and aired on Animal Planet.

Right: Brian Davis (director), Rob McBroom (cast), Martin J. Smith (author of "The Wild Duck Chase"), Adam Grimm (cast), Rebekah Knight (cast), Tim Taylor (cast) and Dee Dee Murry (cast).

photo by Tammy Bowman

photo by Amanda Edwards/Getty Images

Twice a year, the Television Critics Association holds a "Press Tour" at the Beverly Hilton Hotel in Los Angeles, which showcases new and returning shows for hundreds of journalists. Animal Planet flew me out to attend, complete with a private Limo to and from the airport, and a chauffeur holding a sign with my name as I got off the plane. At first, I looked around to see who the other "Murry" was, as that couldn't be for me. I was obviously out of my element and wishing I hadn't just stopped at one of the airport shops to buy a cheese wedge hat that was too big for my suitcase.

I, and the others in the film, were treated to the most luxurious Hotel I'd ever seen. We were part of interviews and photo shoots, and got to meet the General Manager of Animal Planet who was very nice and made me feel at ease, talking about her beloved soft coated wheaten terriers and showing me her necklace with one of the dogs on it. The Hotel was buzzing with people from all walks in the film industry, and separate events in preparation for the big event on stage.I had my own makeup artist, who had also been the makeup artist for Betty White, and got my first professional makeup job. By the time we gathered backstage, I felt like Dorothy Gale, after being buffed and coiffed before meeting the Wizard.

When we finally lined up and walked out on stage, we were met with bright lights and a sea of journalists in the darkened audience. My main goal was to hold it all together and not spit out something inappropriate, so remained as quiet as possible. But when I watched the clip of the documentary on the big screens set up around the massive auditorium, and Hallie's beautiful face came up, my heart about jumped out of my chest with pride. I wished she could have been with me that day and liked to think she was sending me some of her mood lifting zoomies that always brought a smile.

Our 4 year long journey after she went blind was the most incredible and moving experience of my life. Hallie always lived life to the fullest, gracefully leaping all of the bumps in her road along the way and showing me the importance of living in the moment, loving without fear, not letting life rob you of joy and the meaning of true and unconditional love.

She was my inspiration.

My heart and soul.

And my greatest gift.

At the age of 14, she left me, on Christmas Eve. A bright star rising to the heavens on the most Holy of nights. She is in much better hands than mine now and I know this parting is only temporary because I am certain we WILL be together again one day. And I can't wait to see everything she has to show me.

"for we walk by faith, not by sight...."

In the meantime, she decided I needed someone to keep an eye on me. She chose well, a Dennis the Menace in a fuzzy little girl suit. A Havanese named Sophie, who gets into more trouble than a troop of monkeys, is a shameless thief, plays tricks on me and makes me laugh every day.

The very first time I picked her up as a puppy, I held her to my shoulder out of habit and, without thinking, said "give me a Hallie hug".

And she did. In exactly the same way Hallie always did. And she has done it every time I've asked her since.

Hallie had an unusual white streak of hair on her chest that I referred to as her "magic spot."

Sophie shares the same marking, in the same place. Other than her white beard, it's the only other white spot on her body.

People ask me if I will teach Sophie to paint. But that was Hallie's thing. Sophie will carve her own niche in the world. If she has any ideas, she hasn't informed me yet. I am sure that she and Hallie have already been discussing plans. And whatever they are, one thing is for sure. I will be there with her every step of the way, no matter where life takes us.

And I know Hallie will be too.

Made in the USA
Monee, IL
25 May 2022

97015510R00038